How to use this book

Follow the advice, in italics, given for you on each page.
Support the children as they read the text that is shaded in cream.
Praise *the children at every step!*

Detailed guidance is provided in the Read Write Inc. Phonics Handbook

8 reading activities

Children:
- *Practise reading the speed sounds.*
- *Read the green and red words for the story.*
- *Listen as you read the introduction.*
- *Discuss the vocabulary check with you.*
- *Read the story.*
- *Re-read the story and discuss the 'questions to talk about'.*
- *Re-read the story with fluency and expression.*
- *Practise reading the speed words.*

Speed sounds

Consonants *Say the pure sounds (do not add 'uh').*

f	l	m	n	r	s	v	z	sh	th	ng
ff	ll	mm	nn	rr	ss	ve	zz			**(nk)**
			kn				s			

b	c	d	g	h	j	p	**(qu)**	t	w	x	y	ch
bb	k	dd	gg			pp		tt	wh			**(tch)**
	ck											

Vowels *Say the sounds in and out of order.*

at	hen	in	on	up	day	see	high	blow
	head					happy		

zoo	look	car	for	fair	whirl	shout	boy
			door				
			snore				

*Each box contains one sound but sometimes more than one grapheme. Focus graphemes are **circled**.*

Green words

Read in Fred Talk (pure sounds).

drink   wore   shirt   girl   first   squirt

skirt   thirst   dirt

Read in syllables.

bir th`day → birthday       part`y → party   Kirst`y → Kirsty

ketch`up → ketchup       must`ard → mustard

Read the root word first and then with the ending.

start → started   squirt → squirted   stir → stirred

splash → splashed   look → looked

Red words

my   said   so   she   we   me   her   the

5

Vocabulary check

Discuss the meaning (as used in the story) after the children have read each word.

	definition:
squirted	*sprayed*
mustard	*spicy hot sauce*
mashed	*squashed*

Punctuation to note in this story:

Kirsty	*Capital letters for names*
This She So Then	*Capital letters that start sentences*
.	*Full stop at the end of each sentence*
!	*Exclamation mark used to show anger*
...	*Wait and see*

My best shirt

Introduction

What is your favourite party outfit?

Have you ever been naughty at your own party?

The boy in this story is so naughty that he is sent to bed in the middle of his own party!

Story written by Gill Munton
Illustrated by Tim Archbold

This is me in my best shirt.

I wore it at my birthday party.

Mum said it looked smart.

But then I had a food fight

with Kirsty.

She started it.

First, she squirted

ketchup in my hair.

So I squirted mustard

in Kirsty's hair.

Then we felt thirsty.

Kirsty stirred up the lemon drink -

and splashed it on

my best shirt!

Then I mashed up green jelly

and dropped it on her skirt ...

So my best shirt is a bit dirty.

And I'm off to bed at six o'clock.

On my birthday!

Questions to talk about

Re-read the page. Read the question to the children. Tell them whether it is a **FIND IT** *question or* **PROVE IT** *question.*

FIND IT

✓ *Turn to the page*

✓ *Read the question*

✓ *Find the answer*

PROVE IT

✓ *Turn to the page*

✓ *Read the question*

✓ *Find your evidence*

✓ *Explain why*

Page 8:	FIND IT	*What does Mum say about the boy's shirt?*
Page 10:	FIND IT	*How did the food fight start?*
Page 10:	FIND IT	*What was the next thing that happened?*
Page 11:	FIND IT	*What did Kirsty then do?*
Page 11:	PROVE IT	*What did the boy think about this?*
Page 12:	FIND IT	*How did he get his own back on Kirsty?*
Page 13:	PROVE IT	*Mum must be very angry. What do you think she says to her son?*